Books Are Basic

Noel & Judy

the Gospel according to St Lawrence

Larry

Tucson

1985

LAWRENCE CLARK POWELL, 1984

Photograph by John P. Schaefer

BOOKS ARE BASIC
The Essential Lawrence Clark Powell

EDITED BY
John David Marshall

THE UNIVERSITY OF ARIZONA PRESS
TUCSON

LIBRARY OF CONGRESS CATALOGING-IN-PUBLICATION DATA

Powell, Lawrence Clark, 1906–
Books are basic.
Bibliography: p.
1. Books and reading—Quotations, maxims, etc.
2. Library science—Quotations, maxims, etc.
3. Authorship—Quotations, maxims, etc. 4. Powell,
Lawrence Clark, 1906– —Quotations. I. Marshall,
John David. II. Title.
Z1003.P8483 1985 020'.92'4 [B] 85-14099
ISBN 0-8165-0952-2

It is a good thing . . . to read books of quotations. . . . The quotations when engraved upon the memory give you good thoughts. They also make you anxious to read the authors and look for more.

SIR WINSTON S. CHURCHILL
My Early Life: A Roving Commission (1930)

Contents

Foreword

The writings of Lawrence Clark Powell, librarian emeritus of the University of California at Los Angeles, include both fiction and non-fiction. They encompass a diversity of interests and literary forms: music and travel; biography and autobiography; literature and literary criticism; history and geography; the novel and the essay; book reviews and epigraphs; bibliography and librarianship; books and the book trade; forewords and afterwords.

"My Favorite Four-Letter Word" is the title of one of his best essays, and his passion for what that word represents dominates his writings. Much of what he has written has in time found its way into the format represented by that favorite four-letter word, which is, of course, *book*.

The variety of formats in which his works have appeared is almost equal to the diversity of his literary interests. His articles and essays have appeared in octavos, miniature books, at least one "giant miniature," limited editions of fine printing, mimeographed publications, broadsides, and journal articles in reprint and offprint.

The late Joseph Henry Jackson once observed that the essays of Lawrence Clark Powell are characterized by a "pleasant, easy-rolling, gently humorous and always eminently sensible style." To "eminently sensible" should be added "highly personal," for his style is that too.

Author-librarians are rarely represented in books of quotations. Most of what they write is neither very memorable nor very quotable. To include Lawrence Clark Powell in this group of librarian-authors would be "terminological inexactitude" of the highest order. He is the exception. In his writings there are sentences and paragraphs which are memorable and quotable: Quotations on books and reading; on libraries, librarians, librarianship; on writers and writing. Scattered through his various essays and articles are autobiographical references. These provide another kind of memorable and frequently quotable quotation: Lawrence Clark Powell on Lawrence Clark Powell.

For some thirty years now I have been a Powell collector—of his works and his words. *Books Are*

Basic is the product of this collecting interest. When I began a folder of "LCP quotes" a goodly number of years ago, I never expected that it would one day become a book.

I very much hope that this book of quotations will lure readers to seek out in bookstores and libraries the books of librarianship's finest modern essayist. Books such as *Islands of Books*, *The Alchemy of Books*, *A Passion for Books*, *Books in My Baggage*, *Books West Southwest*, *Bookman's Progress*, *The Little Package*, and *Fortune and Friendship*.

For asking me to undertake the compilation of a collection of quotations from the writings of Lawrence Clark Powell, I thank Jack Walsdorf of Blackwell North America, Inc. He made my day on that afternoon in October last year when he called to talk with me about this project.

To Lawrence Clark Powell for giving this project his blessing and approval go sincere thanks of course. But most of all I thank him for writing the books, articles, essays, reviews from which I have drawn these quotations.

JOHN DAVID MARSHALL

On Books and Reading

*T*HE importance of books is that they are the best means man has found to forward his ideas. Books are more lasting than individual men. *At the Heart of the Matter* (1957: 1)

. . . books are basic, books are best, books are to be read and shared, world without end.
The Little Package (1964: 23)

Books are our best commodity because a good book is timeless and translatable and speaks with an undying voice. A technical report is to a book as the leaf is to the tree. Books are to read and to talk about because they are all of man—head, heart, and soul. Technical reports *can* change the world, and have, witness those of Lawrence, Teller, and Oppenheimer, but when they are classified and unspeakable, what then?
UCLA Librarian (1959: 42)

He who would break out of the daily straight-jacket must seek his own time and place of truth. Books help. Books are triggers to shoot us free, are bombs to blow us up and away.
Southwestern Book Trails (1963: 36)

. . . books, books, books in all their aspects, in form and spirit, their physical selves and what reading releases from their hieroglyphic pages, in their sight and smell, in their touch and feel to the questing hand, and in the intellectual music which they sing to thoughtful brain and loving heart, books are to me the best of all symbols, the realest of all reality.

The Alchemy of Books (1954: 21)

Read by sunlight, lamplight, or, as Lincoln did, by firelight, the book is still the best way man has found to record and transmit his knowledge.   *A Passion for Books* (1958: 20)

Books themselves need no defense. Their spokesmen come and go, their readers live and die, they remain constant.   *The Alchemy of Books* (1954: ix)

One book, such as the Bible or Plato or Shakespeare, may contain the essence of man's ideas, and thus though the world itself be lost, if that one book survive and one man and woman live to read it, then is the future secured.

At the Heart of the Matter (1957: 2)

One good book leads to a dozen others.

Books in My Baggage (1960: 81)

Books are librarians' prime commodity and it is their prime responsibility to know this commodity. They must recognize books as mortal things of cloth and paper and ink, which need loving care if they are to survive; and then again they must recognize them also as superior beings, things of truth and dream, greater and more lasting than their custodians are.

Books in My Baggage (1960: 80)

An old book which bears no plate or mark of ownership is a book only half alive.

Jones's *The Human Side of Bookplates* (1951: xii)

What single book would one choose to be cast away with on a desert island? My choice would be a Webster's Unabridged, that great mother of books, that matrix from which one man delivers *Finnegan's Wake*, another *A Shropshire Lad*. What a glorious prospect—to be alone on an island, with an opportunity to sit back against a banana tree, and read all the way from aardvark to zymurgy!   *The Alchemy of Books* (1954: 153–54)

Books, I say, are truly alchemical agents; for they, more than any other of man's creations, have the power of transforming something common (meaning you and me as we are most of the time) into something precious (meaning you and me as God meant us to be). Both the physical book, in its format of print and binding, and the essential book, in what its words say and mean, by tones and overtones, have this power in a measure unknown to any other of the so-called library media.   *The Alchemy of Books* (1954: 154)

Of all men's children, books are the most lasting.   *At the Heart of the Matter* (1957: 2)

What makes a book great, a so-called classic, is its quality of always being modern, of its author, though he be long dead, continuing to speak to each new generation.   *The Little Package* (1964: 235)

A good bookman regards books as part of his essential traveling equipment. . . . A good book speaks to one in these words, "Everyman, I will go with thee, and be thy guide, In thy most need to go by thy side." And the wise man listens.

Books in My Baggage (1960: 197)

6

People turn to books for all that books hold for people: knowledge and power, distraction, delight, strength and solace.

The Little Package (1964: 36)

. . . the Little Package. What's in it? Dynamite, to blow you up. Honey, to heal you. A fire opal, for beauty. A scarf of colored silk. Sea shells for music. River sand to filter impurities. Rose petals. Leaves of grass. . . . You know what I mean by "Little Package." Books, of course.

The Little Package (1964: 230–31)

If you want to maintain your security and self-assurance, stay away from certain books. Don't open that Little Package, if you are afraid of being blown sky-high, or lulled to dreams, or dazzled by beauty. Pandora's Box had nothing on a book.

The Little Package (1964: 232)

Efforts at censorship only serve to advertise a book.

The Little Package (1964: 236)

The dangerous books are not the ones the censors try to suppress. . . . The dangerous books of American literature are about such things as whales, grass, a pond in the woods, a raft on the river. Poems, essays, novels. Beware of these little packages, these bombs in sheep's binding. They slide down the throat, then explode in the stomach, whereas such obviously revolutionary books as *Das Kapital* and *Mein Kampf* stick in the throat and, if they are swallowed, produce indigestion from their lumpiness. Their time has passed. They are dead.

The Little Package (1964: 232)

The presence of rich stocks of British books in American libraries is to me one of the best guarantees that our cultures will remain linked forever. What is needed now is for more British libraries to collect American books. There should be a free flow of books both ways between our countries. Unlike men, books are ambassadors that never die. *Books in My Baggage* (1960: 119)

If we are to triumph in the world struggle, it will be because our ideas, not our arms, are the strongest; and books are the best packages man has ever found to hold his ideas. . . . The best way to tell our story is by the great books of our American heritage. . . . You moon travelers, put

Walden in your pocket, if the Air Force will let you; it bulks less, yet weighs more, than *War and Peace.* Hide *Huckleberry Finn* on your person; it will export better than *Crime and Punishment.*

The Little Package (1964: 237)

A book is one of the most patient of all man's inventions. Centuries mean nothing to a well-made book. It awaits its destined reader, come when he may, with eager hand and seeing eye. Then occurs one of the great examples of union, that of a man with a book, pleasurable, sometimes fruitful, potentially world-changing, simple; and in a public library . . . without cost to the reader.   *Know Your Library* (1958–59: 4)

The study of a culture calls for a knowledge of and a feel for every aspect of that period. Bindings tell us much of the people for whom they were made. Ornate blind-stamped pigskin Bibles of Gutenberg's time, the *Pilgrim's Progress* in sober sheep, the yellowbacks of the Victorians, modern French bindings of introverted intricacy of pattern, and the honest buckram which preserves today's periodicals—these are more than utilitarian; they are also evidences of the needs

9

and the nature of a given time; and to junk them all for their texts on film is an indication of insensitive sterility.   *Rub-Off* (1958: 3)

There is the magic which makes encyclopedias the potent things they are. Imagine, all knowledge in a single set of books! All human ailments and cures. The alchemist's secret, the philosopher's stone, Aladdin's lamp, the essence of life itself. And, in children's and young people's encyclopedias, the essence further distilled to its quintessence; complexities simplified, professional language and jargon eschewed, knowledge brought down to a basic level so that primary learning can occur with only the book as teacher.
New York Times Book Review (1967: 68)

. . . the book is the common key to the mind and heart, no matter the language in which it is printed, and readers and librarians are a universal brotherhood.   *A Passion for Books* (1958: 214)

. . . there is no substitute for direct contact with books, and that bibliographical mastery comes from the factual and optical as well as from the intellectual sense—plus a bit of serendipity.
Library Quarterly (1976: 463)

To be a classic a book need not have unanimous or even majority acceptance.

Southwest Classics (1974: 89)

Unless their use by readers brings them to life, books are indeed dead things.

Wilson Library Bulletin (1970: 384)

By *magnetic field* a scientist means that field of force around a magnet wherein a piece of iron, though not in contact with the magnet, will be attracted to it. . . . Books also are magnets, with the power to attract people. A single book may have this magnetic force, and when hundreds and thousands of books are brought together in bookshops and libraries, their power is increased, so that such a place of bookish concentration possesses an irresistible attraction for readers and collectors.

A Passion for Books (1958: 22–23)

Some books are to be read in an hour, and returned to the shelf; others require a lifetime to savor their richness. Such books should be owned in personal copies, to travel with and to sleep beside—the most fruitful of all companions. Only your bookseller can consummate such a union of book and reader.

Know Your Library (1955: 4)

Bookmen know that the really rare books are the ones nobody wants but you.

Books in My Baggage (1960: 86)

Bookshops are the best places to meet and learn from book collectors.   *The Little Package* (1964: 42)

Sociologists would find, if they made a study (and they probably have), that there is a correlation between the cultural level in a community and the number of bookshops it supports.

Books West Southwest (1957: 124)

No city is civilized that does not support a variety of bookshops.   *The Little Package* (1964: 196)

Librarians have much to learn from booksellers. There is a great book on this subject—David A. Randall's *Dukedom Large Enough*—anecdotal memoirs of his life, first as bookseller with Scribner's, New York, and for the last twenty years, as the first librarian of the Lilly Library at Indiana University.   *Wilson Library Bulletin* (1970: 387)

This total stimulation of book-collecting is what

makes it such an irresistible passion. The hunting of books in every kind of shop or in dealers' catalogs, the capture and the carrying them away to one's den where the prize can be inspected in privacy, and then the overtones that follow reading—there is no magic like it, no enchantment on earth as fatal.   *A Passion for Books* (1958: 62–63)

Every librarian should have a few collecting hobbies, either of favorite subjects or authors.
Books in My Baggage (1960: 79)

Lend not your books. Don't try to compete with the public library.   *California Monthly* (1963: 19)

We are the children of a technological age. We have found streamlined ways of doing much of our routine work. Printing is no longer the only way of reproducing books. Reading them, however, has not changed; it is the same as it has always been, since Callimachus administered the great library in Alexandria.
Books in My Baggage (1960: 75)

Reading books is good, re-reading good books is better.   *California Classics* (1971: xii)

We rarely discover a book on our own. We read about it, or are told of it by a friend, a librarian, a bookseller, or a reviewer. Help is needed to discern the pearls of literature in the trash-heap of our age of permissive print.

California Classics (1971: 224)

"No pleasure has ever been found equal to that of reading good books." I believe this to be true, and have built my life on the belief. The more complex, demanding, and exhausting our civilization becomes . . . the more potent is the good medicine stored in books.   *Know Your Library* (1958–59: 4)

A book truly lives only by being read.

Southwest Classics (1974: 191)

Books will be read? Of course they will, forever and always. . . . There is no substitute for reading.   *A Passion for Books* (1958: 209)

We read books for various reasons—for facts, for fiction, to go deeper into life, to escape from life; and the greatest books are those that most completely satisfy these different needs.

The Three L's (1964: 3)

Reading is done easily, and it is inexpensive. . . .
Once you have learned to read, nature takes care
of the rest. There is no formal procedure, routine, or protocol about reading. Do it wherever
you are, wearing what you will, alone or together, and if you choose, disbelieving every
word the author has written. If anyone in the Library should mistakenly ask your reason for
wanting this book or that, ignore him. Your reading is your private affair. In the United States of
America, there is no power on earth to compel
you to read this, or to prevent you from reading
that.   *Know Your Library* (1958–59: 4)

Every book has its inevitable time and place to be
read.   *Southwest Classics* (1974: 121)

There is a power in some books to evoke the time
and the place of their first reading, when by
merely giving a glimpse to their backs they take
us backward to that moment of discovery which
now seems magically inevitable.

Books in My Baggage (1960: 15)

To live is good. To read is good. To blend living
and reading, to experience those wonderful

unions of the time, the place, and the book, is almost unspeakably good.

The Little Package (1964: 247)

The simple act of reading, the way of man with a book, is universal, transcending time and space. . . .   "Books Will Be Read" (1957: 49)

Random reading is delightful reading; browsing, skipping and jumping, reading half a dozen books concurrently, mixing reading and living so that the one heightens and intensifies the other. . . .   *The Alchemy of Books* (1954: 121)

He who lives and reads not is no more alive than he who reads and lives not.

California Monthly (1963: 19)

To merge and become one with life, to increase my understanding and sympathy for people— these are some of my aims in reading.

The Alchemy of Books (1954: 103)

The act of living is well and good, but unless one is a mystic who can break the time barrier, enter the time continuum, and experience past, present and future as one, then for the actual acts of living is he confined to the ever coming, ever going present moment. Only by reading, by what I have called the act of enchantment, can man live in the past, albeit vicariously. Only in books will he find the past usefully preserved. Without books, or their equivalents, man would lead a succession of brilliant, ephemeral moments, without the light and shade which make our recorded past.

Thus, I say, *books determine*.

Southwestern Book Trails (1963: 66)

He who travels and reads not is poor indeed, and he who reads and travels not is only half alive.   *Books in My Baggage* (1960: 203–204)

I do not believe that life holds anything more basic than food, love, and books. Various arrangements of the three are possible, either simultaneously or in sequence. In my experience, however, the two that go best together are eating and reading.

The Magpie Press Typographical Cookbook (1964: 1)

If you detonate easily, be mindful of what you

read. If you already have all the answers, don't bother to read. But if you are hungry and eager, or fed up and bored, feel good and want it to last, feel bad and want it to end, then your library can be your rainbow's end. *Good Reading* (1961: 1)

. . . may there ever be books in your life, for there is life for you in books, the essence of all the lives man has ever lived, from Homer to Hemingway, heroic, tragic, loving, wrapped for your convenience in this Little Package called Book.

The Little Package (1964: 238)

Man has found no better form in which to preserve his ideas than the printed book. It is a neat, compact, well behaved invention; it waits for you, for centuries sometimes. It is there when you want it. You need no apparatus to deal with a book. It slips into your pocket; it fits your hand; it yields to your eye. A book asks no questions of your color or creed or college degree.

At the Heart of the Matter (1957: 2)

How does one find time for books? . . . *One finds time for books by taking it.*

Library Journal (1957: 3160)

Books determine, have determined, will determine our lives, as readers and writers, and for this, let us give thanks.

Books West Southwest (1957: 37)

*On Libraries, Librarians,
and Librarianship*

*M*ERE size does not make a library great. The quality and functional arrangement of the collection, the intelligence and willingness of the staff—these can be present in a small, choice library; and if they are, then that library is a great library, a useful library.   *The Three H's* (1971: 8)

. . . books are the first essential of a library's greatness.   *The Alchemy of Books* (1954: 244)

Do you want facts? Want to prove something? Trying to find yourself, or the opposite, escape from yourself? We've got books for all purposes, for yes and no, for good and bad, black and white, near and far, for and against. . . . something for every student, hurried or not, this intellectual free-for-all called the Library, which finds the books of all times, races, colors, and creeds, stacked peacefully together under one roof.
Know Your Library (1957–58: 3)

. . . libraries are similar to cathedrals, in that they are sources of solace as well as of strength.
Books West Southwest (1957: 141)

23

Take books out of libraries, and they won't need librarians for what's left. Curled-up film in cans, spools of wire and wheels of tape, shining disks and glassy slides—all the so-called nonbook material has its place in the modern library, yes, but not in the center.   *Books in My Baggage* (1960: 182)

No university in the world has ever risen to greatness without a correspondingly great library. . . . When this is no longer true, then will our civilization have come to an end.

At the Heart of the Matter (1957: 4)

Sooner or later everything comes in and goes out of a university library: books on French roulette and the dynamics of turbulent flow, on vector analysis and psychoanalysis, books of missals and on missiles, on flood and drought, law and disorder, books for and against, of good and evil, all free to all, a storehouse as powerful as any uranium stockpile, each volume awaiting the touch of hand, the sight of eye to release its energy.

Books in My Baggage (1960: 148)

What Miller wanted was a book. I looked it up in

the catalog. I charged it out and let him have it. There is the quintessence of library service. You have the book that somebody wants. You let him have it. I don't know how many books UCLA has loaned Henry Miller since that one in 1941. Certainly in the thousands. Every one was returned—with interest. The books, manuscripts, papers, and letters given by him to UCLA and which form the Henry Miller Archive more than counterbalance the value of all that we ever loaned him.

What *was* that one book in 1941? It was a philosophical treatise by the German shoemaker mystic, Jacob Boehme, entitled *Aurora, or the Morning Rednesse*, a title Yeats thought the loveliest ever given to a book.

From the Heartland (1976: 152)

No atomic pile stores more potential energy than a university library, and no university is greater than its library, witness Oxford and Harvard.

The Little Package (1964: 208)

The Library takes the middle road between serving people and conserving books. It collects rare books of the past for immediate use in the present, and at the same time ensures the future a rich legacy by the way it husbands its holdings.

Clark Memorial Library, UCLA,
Director's Report (1958/59: 1)

A library should have as few rules as possible, someone (not a librarian) once said, and break them all whenever necessary.

The Little Package (1964: 18)

. . . the library is one of our few remaining sanctuaries for the individual who when he enters wants to be together with books and not with people. *Know Your Library* (1959–60: 4)

. . . books are fluid, explosive, fissionable objects, packed with the dynamite of change and progress. Conservative and radical can meet in the library on neutral ground. The library is a staging area for social change, yet it is also a sanctuary for those who seek respite from the violence that torments us. *The Abiding Legacy* (1971: 8)

To a library come travellers who thirst and are refreshed, who hunger and are nourished. A library is also a magnet which draws the intellectually curious. In a library one meets people from the four corners of the earth, and both sides of the tracks. The children's room in a public library seems to me fully as hallowed a place as a Sunday School. Paradoxically, the public library is one of the few places left where one can be private.

Arizona Highways (1960: 7)

There exists a sure correlation between the greatness of a university and the importance of its library. I am ready to pay a reward to anyone who can name a major university whose library is undistinguished. It is no accident that Harvard and Oxford, for example, have libraries to match their stature among the universities of the world.

Know Your Library (1954: 4)

. . . fair buildings . . . willing librarians . . . great books, however essential, are not the library. The library is living readers.

Library Journal (1964: 565)

People who use libraries might be classified (librarians love to classify) into three groups: those who know what they want and don't want any help in finding it; those who don't know what they want and want help in finding it; and those who think they know what they want, but don't *really*.   *Know Your Library* (1959–60: 4)

The public comes to the library for the books or the facts; nothing else matters.
                    The Little Package (1964: 21)

The classics of tomorrow can be created at no other time than today.
                    College and Research Libraries (1939: 103)

Libraries should aid living authors of actual or potential greatness, whose works meet no popular success, by buying their books upon publication, and making them available to that small fraction of their patrons who have independent taste and powers of discrimination, and whose book hunger is not dependent upon bibliographic or pedagogic stimuli.
                    Books in My Baggage (1960: 66)

. . . the research library's function is to anticipate demand, and to have on its shelves the complete early works of the obscure poet who years later, perhaps not until after his death, may be recognized as one of the true voices of his time—one whose few hundred lines will be read long after [*Forever*] *Amber* is forgotten.

Books in My Baggage (1960: 65)

. . . every great library's shelves creak under generations of mediocre tomes, and academic studies are not infrequently devoted to works forgotten by all save the catalog and the researcher who threads its million-carded maze.

Books in My Baggage (1960: 65)

In a great library which has amassed and cherishes and makes useful the treasures of our literature, a reader can slip into the time-stream which flows from past, to present, to future, and back again. Once he learns by education to live in this continuum, a man will live no other way, will never be without book in hand.

Landscapes and Bookscapes of California (1958: 15)

If the library is truly the heart of the campus, then its valves must open both in and out. As Dixon Wecter observed, a library should be a blood bank, not a columbarium.

The Alchemy of Books (1954: 244)

It is the obligation of a head librarian . . . to be

unmistakably a librarian, to be a person who is recognizable by his acts and words as one whose business is books, who can answer questions about books, who will take a stand on issues involving books, all without referring the matter to a subordinate, or worse, to a committee.

Library Journal (1957: 3160)

Good [library] administration requires strength, perception, and recognition in equal amounts. It also helps to soak regularly in a strong saline solution in order to toughen the hide.

Service or Organization (1974: 2)

To try to separate administration and management would seem to me merely an exercise in semantics, and to seek to separate [library] administration and books, tragic.

Library Journal (1957: 3159)

The monologue is most people's favorite form of conversation.   *Wilson Library Bulletin* (1959: 420)

It is foolish . . . to debate which is more important in a library: books or people. Both are essential, and both should be in constant equilibrium. . . . Good administration in a library is the attainment of a gracious and economical union of books and people. To do this successfully calls for knowledge of both.   *Library Journal* (1957: 3159)

I have no respect for the research degree program as preparation for administration, nor for any course in administration which omits books. . . . Nor have I respect for library administrators whose published writings and reports give no indication that books are their business. Their language is managerial, theoretical, abstract. They could be administrators of anything on earth— supermarket, bank, shoestore, cemetery. Their feeling for books and people is impersonal, scientific, objective, objectionable.

Library Journal (1957: 3160)

A profession will go no farther than its leaders take it along the road of service to humanity. The supreme goal of administration is to lead, and if one would have followers, then must he be able to inspire others to follow him, to do as he does.

A library administrator could wish for no better epitaph than, *He was a leader, and a reader.*

Library Journal (1957: 3161)

. . . a library administrator should be recognizably a librarian, no matter the time of day or year.
Library Journal (1957: 3160)

I could no more pass a library without going in than I could keep from books and bananas for breakfast. Library is my synonym for sanctuary.
Library Journal (1962: 514)

. . . the building is the least important factor in a library situation, occupying last place after books and staff.

Books are of course the most important, for a roomful of books, without any attendant, to which knowing readers have access, *is* a library. But when there is more than a roomful, when there are stacks of books in the complex arrangement of a great public or research library, then the people in charge, those with the keys, are gods indeed. And if the prospective reader is unknowing and in need of help and the librarians are unreading, unwilling, gadgety, and ambitious only for self-advancement through the fringes of benefit to the throne of administration, then pity the poor reader—he is better off in drugstore and supermarket.
A Passion for Books (1958: 209)

The Library is for books, the books are for you. . . . Read one, read a hundred, a thousand. They are unrationed, and they are fully packed with pleasure and with knowledge, yours free for the reading. *Know Your Library* (1958–59: 4)

Give us librarians who have a passion for books, who are bookmen by birth and by choice, by education, profession, and hobby. Properly disciplined, this passion for books is the greatest asset a librarian can have. *The Alchemy of Books* (1954: 91)

The good librarian recognizes a threefold obligation—to the past for its heritage, to the present for the support which maintains him and his charges, and to the future which may flower in a Montaigne, a Cervantes, a Goethe, to the ennoblement of mankind. *The Alchemy of Books* (1954: 93)

. . . the two chief attributes of a good librarian are that he be a reader of books, and a servant of those in need of help.

A Passion for Books (1958: 209)

To be a good librarian means a life of dedicated hard work. *Library Journal* (1964: 564)

A good librarian is both extrovert and introvert, is both organization and anti-organization. It is a fine art to hold these opposites in harmony. To be a good librarian is hard, demanding, exhausting, and also joyful, rewarding, refreshing.

Library Journal (1964: 565)

Booksellers and librarians trade in immortal merchandise. They are in it together, and there is one name for them both. I pen it with pride. The name is Bookman. Long may they flourish!

A Passion for Books (1958: 78)

The good librarian is a universalist, a generalist, rather than a specialist. He will know some useful thing about almost everything, ancient and modern, local, regional, and national; about all aspects of culture, the arts and the sciences.

The good librarian reads the daily newspaper, the dictionary, the encyclopedia, the pharmacopoeia. He helps the individual maintain private health; he helps the masses maintain public health.

The Three H's (1971: 6)

Give us more literate librarians in fine libraries,

and the reading of books will be measureless. There is hope in this prospect, and joy.

A Passion for Books (1958: 215)

. . . a good librarian is approachable, affirmative, inquiring, both a reader and a handler of books.

The Little Package (1964: 20)

Believers and doers are what we need—faithful librarians who are humble in the presence of books. To enter a library, no matter its kind or size, is to enter the heart of the whirlwind. To be in a library is one of the purest of all experiences. This awareness of a library's unique, even sacred nature is what should be instilled in our neophytes. *A Passion for Books* (1958: 204)

Not a day should pass but that every librarian, in every library on earth, regardless of how high he is in the administrative hierarchy, should handle books. . . . When a librarian loses physical contact with books, his strength goes. He becomes indistinguishable from administrators anywhere—of stores, hospitals, banks, cemeteries. And he becomes a foreigner to those librarians—

35

still in a majority, thank God—who live, touch, and breathe books, eagerly, lovingly, usefully, rewardingly. And who read books that they may know more, to be able better to serve people, or who read books for simple delight, in order that the world, at once cruel and kind, be made more bearable, more adorable.

A Passion for Books (1958: 215)

A good librarian today must be able to operate both mechanically and humanistically, must cope with machines and with men. . . .

Library Journal (1964: 562)

. . . when a librarian loses physical contact with books, then he is no longer a strong librarian.

The Little Package (1964: 20)

What makes a librarian professional, in my book, is his devotion this side of fanaticism to the cordial service of people who want and need books. A good librarian knows, serves, believes. He ignores clock and calendar, and the caste which deifies the administrator and degrades the book-handling (and reading) rank and file of untouchables.   *The Little Package* (1964: 19)

What is it that gives a librarian status as member of a profession? Competence in acquiring, classifying, cataloging, and housing the contents of a library? Planning, construction, and operation of a library building? Recruitment, training, and employment of personnel? Belonging to associations and committees and attending conferences?

None of these. All are library housekeeping. They are important, and the librarians who practice them are indispensable. Good housekeeping is basic. . . . As a library user, I take housekeeping for granted, and am concerned only when it is bad housekeeping. In using a research library, I want to talk with someone—I don't care what his title is or where he was educated for librarianship, if at all—who knows what that library has that may help me; where it is; and why it is important.

Wilson Library Bulletin (1970: 387–388)

The public expects two things of a librarian: that he be bookish and that he be cordial.

The Little Package (1964: 19)

A good librarian is not a social scientist, an educationalist, a documentalist, a retrievalist, or an automaton. A good librarian is a librarian: a person with good health and warm heart, trained by study and seasoned by experience to catalyze books and people.   *The Little Package* (1964: 22)

The good librarian is both priest and doctor.
Library Journal (1962: 514)

Earth, air, fire, and water are the elements of physical matter. Curiosity, perception, courage, service, and dedicated belief are the elements of a good librarian. O Lord, help us be such!
The Little Package (1964: 35)

. . . the three h's. What are they? First, *head*. A good librarian knows, has knowledge, an inquiring mind. Second, *hands*. A good librarian can handle books, strongly, surely, delicately. Is even a binder. Third, *heart*. A good librarian feels loving toward people, is motivated to serve others, is a yea-sayer.   *The Little Package* (1964: 62)

As librarians we have close and constant access to the world's knowledge. We are thus privileged. We are also obliged, I say, to be informed, not only about the physical nature of books and librarianship, the techniques and the housekeeping required of us, we must also penetrate the covers of books to the contents. We must know what it is that readers seek and where to find it.

The Three H's (1971: 5)

Write to be understood, speak to be heard, read to grow. . . . When asked who you are, reply with two one-letter words, one two-letter word, plus one longer word, which go to make the declarative sentence, *I am a librarian*.

The Little Package (1964: 44–45)

To know books and to know people, and to fuse that knowledge into an inseparable course of action, is the highest good to which a librarian can attain, and to such a fusion every good librarian's life is dedicated. *AB: Bookman's Yearbook* (1957: 44)

. . . professional status is contingent upon giving, not getting. Many library school graduates and working librarians are not and never will be professional people, as long as they are 8 to 5, 40-hour workers, and are self-confessedly too busy to read. *Library Journal* (1957: 3161)

In the literature on librarian status-seekers, I read much of what librarians expect to achieve in the status package, namely longer vacations and sabbatical leaves. I read less of what they are prepared to pay for it. *Wilson Library Bulletin* (1970: 386)

Involvement in administration does not increase knowledge of a library's contents or zeal to serve its users. *Wilson Library Bulletin* (1970: 386)

. . . the bad public image of librarians—an old chestnut if there ever was one. We all know what the image is: repressed, timid, conservative, clerical, and so on. We all know many such librarians. We know them well: *ourselves*. All of us are somewhat inhibited, fearful, wedded to the status quo, dependent upon daily routines. As human beings, we will always be somewhat less than paragons of efficiency and virtue.

Library Journal (1964: 562)

As a library user, what do I expect of librarians in public service? That they be able and willing, that their knowledge be accompanied by zeal and skill to share it. I want them available, on or near the firing line, not in a committee meeting or gone to a conference.   *Wilson Library Bulletin* (1970: 386)

. . . I have observed that librarians have become increasingly addicted to committees and conferences. The higher the person's rank, the more apt he is to be elsewhere.

Service or Organization (1974: 1)

A library whose staff are concerned with the number of hours they work is a library without distinction.   *Service or Organization* (1974: 2)

An incalculable number of working hours has been spent by librarians in search of faculty rank. . . . There is only one way for librarians to achieve faculty rank, and that is by doing what the faculty does, that is, teach, research, write, and publish. And too close an identification with faculty can result in librarians suffering the miseries as well as the grandeurs.

Service or Organization (1974: 3)

Let's forget this nonsense about a librarian being well-rounded. Life is too short. There are no more Leonardos or Humboldts, not to mention

John Cotton Danas or Justin Winsors. People must specialize to thrive; let librarians specialize in books and library service.

Library Journal (1962: 514)

Isn't this the heart of the matter, the very essence of library service? That we have what is needed, for him who needs it, in the time of his need. And to know what we have, who we are, and how to do what we must do for those who need us, be they poor or rich or neither, and in this knowledge to be proud, a pride derived from service to others. Then and only then will we deserve the word "professional." It is all profoundly simple. Let us not complicate it.   *ALA Bulletin* (1965: 648)

If there isn't a bookstore in your community, you are lacking one of the hallmarks of civilization. Church, school, library, park, bookstore—the essentials for cultural living.

California Monthly (1963: 19)

The first essential element for a fruitful relationship between librarian and bookseller is *sympathy*. Each party must feel sympathetic toward the other, must like one another, must sense a human kinship, must feel and act friendly. An impersonal, cut and dried relationship will produce a certain amount of business, but it will not result in the dividends and bonuses of a relationship which goes deeper than dollars and cents. . . .

Allied to sympathy as a necessary essential of a fruitful relationship is *understanding*. The librarian must understand the bookseller's problems of source and supply, of overhead and staff, of profit in order to survive. For his part, the bookseller must understand the librarian's problems of budget, procedure, and institutional limitations. . . .

A third element is *trust*. Its presence in both parties means that business can be done swiftly and without tedious correspondence and dickering and suspicious safeguards. A word or two on the phone or in person can mean the consummation of a deal, small or large—if the parties trust each other's integrity and good faith. . . .

This brings me to the final, and in some ways the most important element of all, that of *knowledge*. In order to make a rapid decision, which booksellers always seek, the librarian must know his own collection, that of his neighbors, and the importance of the material being offered. . . .

There is an equal responsibility for the bookseller to know not only his own stock, but the collections and needs of the libraries which he serves or hopes to serve. Again this means time and effort and study. . . .

It boils down to these elements: *sympathy, understanding, trust*, and *knowledge*. If they are present in the community of bookseller-librarian, the two parties, and all learning, will flourish and be fruitful.   "Elements of Fruitfulness" (1956: 2, 5)

In spite of the fact that we librarians are collectively the custodians of millions of volumes, we should also collect our own private libraries, be they ever so small. *The Alchemy of Books* (1954: 125)

Some utopian day, when I have more money than books, and providing I can engage the Los Angeles Colosseum, I am going to invite all the librarians in the land to meet together, for the first time, to talk merely about the two things we all have in common: books and people.

UCLA Librarian (1956: 119)

Library literature is barren of material on reading and collecting by librarians. Library conferences are mostly given over to problems as keepers of books. It is time for a revolution, for a return to fundamentals, the most elementary of which is the truth that books are written and published first of all to be read; and that librarians, a favored people who hold custody of the world's stock of books, should be the most avid readers on earth.   *Books in My Baggage* (1960: 79)

The ideal librarian will regard books as teachers *par excellence*, remembering, for example, how they rather than any school or university taught the young Lincoln. *The Alchemy of Books* (1954: 95)

No teacher is so bad that a student can't learn from him. The present concern with evaluating teachers seems to me largely a waste of time. To declare that students and teachers are co-equals is absurd.   *Wilson Library Bulletin* (1970: 386)

There are two kinds of reading which librarians should do: one for instruction and intellectual growth, the other for entertainment and delight; and to me they are of equal importance.
                    The Alchemy of Books (1954: 120)

The book is the best form man has yet found to preserve and transmit his ideas. It is every librarian's sacred obligation to know all there is to know about these practical and sometimes beautiful idea forms called books.   *Rub-Off* (1958: 3)

Librarians should read the books they live with, and keep their response to them always direct, personal, intense, and simple. Books should be read with body and soul, and not with the brain alone. . . .   *Books in My Baggage* (1960: 80)

How absurd to proclaim librarianship a science! It is an artful craft, a crafty art, to be practiced with a trinity of talents: hands, head, and heart.
     The Little Package (1964: 19)

. . . nothing in librarianship is more basic than writing and writers, the process and the people who produce information. . . .

Recently I saw a copy of the proceedings of a workshop on public libraries. . . . The proceedings fill more than a hundred pages. In those pages there is no mention by anyone of a specific book or of those transcendent acts of writing and reading which are the blood and the bone and the marrow of librarianship.

Am I saying that it should have been a workshop on writing and reading? No. Although that wouldn't be a bad thing for librarians to do. I *am* saying that it is shocking that librarians could speak for three days and a hundred pages without someone, somehow, perhaps unconsciously, once referring to books, to a book, to any book. It's like a workshop of clergymen who never refer to God.   *ALA Bulletin* (1965: 644/646)

. . . the great simplicities of humane librarianship—that books are basic, that people are good, and that bringing the two together, so that books are made more useful and people more fruitful, is one of the most exciting and rewarding experiences on earth.   *A Passion for Books* (1958: 184)

Librarianship should be as consuming a calling as the ministry and medicine, to which its servants dedicate and give their lives, and in the giving find themselves, renewed and reborn even as they are consumed.   *A Passion for Books* (1958: 167)

To me librarianship lies somewhere between art and craft—it is an artful craft, say, or a crafty art— a black art, I sometimes think, when I lose my way in the maze of a large card catalog.
    The Alchemy of Books (1954: 153)

Central in every library and central in my philosophy and practice of librarianship are books.

Books West Southwest (1957: 5)

Librarianship has been invaded by some people who, if they read books, do it secretly and keep quiet about it afterward. How ignorant these barbarians are of one of the fundamental truths of reading: people who love books love to tell others about them. Anyone who is properly grounded in librarianship—that is, who has worked on a public desk in a library—knows this basic truth: that readers like to share their enthusiasms.

Books West Southwest (1957: 27)

More of the advances in librarianship are due to individual genius than to committees. . . .

The Little Package (1964: 38)

If librarianship is to attain recognition as a profession, there must be more awareness by librarians of the principles of dedicated giving which distinguish a profession from a trade or a craft. This awareness withers under the intense focus of specialization. Let us beware of subdividing ourselves out of professional existence. There are a few strong old words in the language which are weakened when modified, and killed when replaced by fancier words. Such words are *minister*, *doctor*, *lawyer*, and—*librarian*.

Library Journal (1957: 3172)

If one were to rank the professions by the degree of dedicated giving they require of their members, . . . I would place ministry and medicine at the top, followed by librarianship and law.

Library Journal (1957: 3161)

Books such as [*Old and Rare: Thirty Years in the Book Business* by Leona Rostenberg and Madeleine B. Stern (1974)] . . . could help to restore humanistic and bibliographical values to a library world obsessed by acronymic nonsense, endless reorganizations, "goals and objectives," and other presently fashionable nonsense.

Library Quarterly (1976: 463–64)

The respect I have for librarians . . . is determined by the extent to which they are identified with the ideas that have made us a great nation—the ideas of individual liberty and social responsibility—and by their willingness to take a public stand whenever necessary to champion these ideas when they are threatened. . . . They will recognize and proclaim that the sacred American ideas of freedom, tolerance and justice have been enunciated in and transmitted by and are always available in *books*—books that are to be borrowed from public libraries and to be bought in supermarkets and drugstores. The books of Tom Paine and Jefferson, of Franklin, Thoreau, Whitman, Emerson, Mark Twain, Carl Sandburg, Robert Frost, J. Frank Dobie, on down to the writings of that reading man in the White House [John F. Kennedy]. This is my idea of good librarianship.

Special Libraries (1961: 299)

In this area of book substitutes we suffer from the national mania for naming things as a substitute for action. In health it means calling it a virus or an allergy. In education this takes the form of adding a course and giving it a number. In administration it means appointing another committee. In librarianship, statistics have replaced scholarship as the collar on the top dogs.

UCLA/AAUP (1959: 5)

To join or not to join is not the question. To me the question is how can a librarian *not* join the associations which hold his profession together. It is not a question of money. . . . Library association dues are probably the lowest of all the professional groups. People who economize on dues do not always live with corresponding abstemiousness, eschewing beer and bonbons. It is a matter of relative values.

UCLA Librarian (1960: 36)

. . . I persistently believe that in librarianship books are basic, that books determine; and that any course of study which minimizes books is worthless. *Books West Southwest* (1957: 26)

Seek that secret way of lengthening the 24-hour day. And live by the Three H's of good librarianship—by your hands, head, and heart. Remember this though—library sainthood is conferred only posthumously.

Service or Organization (1974: 6)

Let us then be both proud and humble in the practice of our art, for it is an ancient art, a noble art, which serves man in all that he does and would do. It is the art of librarianship in which . . . books are basic. *The Alchemy of Books* (1954:172–73)

On Writers and Writing

*T*HE works of great writers have many uses. They educate the young, cement friendships, or lie placidly as reservoirs to which a man in need can return again and again at different stages in his life.   *Islands of Books* (1951: 71)

. . . the life of a creative writer is not lost when he dies, but is transfused into his book.

Good Reading (1961: 1)

All generalities about writers are suspect. And yet one keeps making them, such as The Place of a Writer's Birth is not Intrinsically Meaningful, or A Writer's Creative Arc is a Good Approach to an Understanding of his Work, or Popular Success is Bad for a Writer.   *Southwest Classics* (1974: 57)

Casanova's *Memoirs* actually form an encyclopedia of Europe in the eighteenth century. His life covered three-quarters of the century, he traveled everywhere, knew everyone, did everything; and when he was sixty years old settled down as—of all things—librarian to a Bohemian count. Then to relieve the boredom of his final dozen years Casanova employed his prodigious memory and fluent pen to write the story of the first forty-seven years of his life. To corrupt Shaw's epigram on teachers, as long as Casanova could, he did; and when he arrived at the age when he couldn't, he wrote.   *Books in My Baggage* (1960: 27)

Writing lasts only when it receives life from the individual. The gift to breathe life into prose is given only to a few.   *The Little Package* (1964: 41)

. . . One morning [February 7, 1951] we heard Churchill from seats in the Strangers' Gallery. There he was, the old warrior, leading the fight that was to return him to power six months later, a bludgeon in one hand, a rapier in the other; and in the political passion that moved him the spoken language sparkled and thundered. What joy to hear English when used to the full advantage of our treasured tongue.

The Alchemy of Books (1954: 82)

Churchill is an old lion, magnificent, formidable, and of course incomparably eloquent.

Librarian-on-Leave (1952: 24)

Style cannot be hidden in a book. It will appear

on every page, in every paragraph and sentence. Without style no book can live more than a season or two; with it, forever.

The Alchemy of Books (1954: 102)

Writing is a solitary occupation. Family, friends, and society are the natural enemies of the writer. He must be alone, uninterrupted, and slightly savage if he is to sustain and complete an undertaking. Quoted in *Hide and Seek* by Jessamyn West (1973: 132)

"Bookscape" means to me the thoughts and feelings evoked when I see a landscape which has become so wedded to a writer's book about it that no divorce of the two is possible. Wessex and Hardy, Shropshire and Housman, the Border Country and Scott, Florence and Browning, Dublin and Joyce. . . .

Books in My Baggage (1960: 169)

To infuse a sense of excitement into prose is necessary, if that prose is going to excite readers. How is this done? Here we are back at the mysterious heart of the matter. To be excited is commonplace; to write prose which is alive and elec-

tric and communicative is rare, calling for
nothing less than mastery of language.

Books in My Baggage (1960: 239–40)

I like books with a feeling for language as well as
for landscape, books with those qualities which
unite to form style: perception, emotion, preci-
sion—style, that fusion of the elements of individual character which results in the distinction
of a writer and his work, which makes the difference between literature and journalism.

Southwestern Book Trails (1963: x)

It takes the life and death of many little writers to
fertilize the land, to build up layers of nourishment, deep down into which the roots of a great
writer can penetrate for nourishment.

Landscapes and Bookscapes of California (1958: 13)

Writing comes hard, the more so the smaller the
space to be filled. Each word on a page of stone-
ground prose should carry its load of meaning
and music. Many books and articles are published
and there is weariness of the eyes; and yet as librarians we should not bite the books we shelve.
Persistent is he who can meet a monthly deadline;

thick-skinned who offers his prose to public
arrows.   *Library Journal* (1962: 60)

To achieve lasting literature, fictional or factual,
a writer needs perceptive vision, absorptive ca-
pacity, and creative strength.

A Southwestern Century (1958: vii)

If a writer would transform . . . landscapes with
people into landscapes with books, he must sink
roots into its sandy soil, send up feelers into its
clear air. He must try to think clearly, to feel
deeply, to write honestly. If he is fortunate he will
make a living, but his work will never be any
more essentially clear and deep and honest than
he himself is, and he will be judged finally not for
how many copies his books have sold, but for
what they have done to enrich the lives of their
readers, now and in time to come.

Books in My Baggage (1960: 241–42)

If land has determined books, then have books
also exalted land. Unions forceful and tender have
been consummated between writers and a region
as magnificent as any on earth.

Southwest Classics (1974: 3)

Seek essences, enduring things, touchstones, and symbols; try to re-create in prose what makes this country so increasingly meaningful and necessary to one. Altitude, distance, color, configuration, history, and culture—in them dwell the essential things, but they must be extracted. "Crack the rock if so you list, bring to light the amethyst." Costs nothing to try. Some have succeeded . . . proving that it is possible. So stand books on the shelf, hang up maps, gaze in the turquoise ball, finger the fragment of red adobe from Pecos, reload the blue Scripto, take a fresh yellow pad, then sit down and see what comes.

Books in My Baggage (1960: 214)

A teacher of writing should lead the student to one of two resolutions: to become a better writer, or to give up writing.

Books in My Baggage (1960: 238)

Landscape with books. And this is why I do not plan to emigrate to the moon or to Venus. No books, at least in recognizable form, have enriched their landscapes, and without books no landscape, however beautiful in itself, can match one which a writer has made into a bookscape.

Books in My Baggage (1960: 179)

I can speak of my own criterion for judging whether or not a book is good or bad. I ask of it a single question, From how deep and true an impulse did it spring? Was it written merely to shock? Only to make money? Or was it written to create something more perfect and more lasting than the life experience from which it came?

You, John Milton (1966: 12)

What is a classic? It could be defined as a book read by more than a single generation. What gives a book long life? Style, I say. And what is style? I see it as a mysterious fusion of fact and imagination, of vision and vigor, present in a writer's mastery of language. If this occurs—and it does so only with unpredictable infrequency—then the result has lasting power to attract and to hold readers, whether the work be novel, poem, narrative essay, or history. *California Classics* (1971: ix)

What do I mean by a classic? Simply the quality of excellence, which leads to a book living on to be read by more than one generation of readers. This quality is derived from several sources: vitality, authority, personality, vision, all of which combine mysteriously to form what is called style. . . . Style is the firing up of the English language until it incandesces but does not melt.

The Untarnished Gold, the Immutable Treasure (1970: 5)

Part of genius is the writer's ability to read the road signs that lead in the right direction, and to take the way to the promised land where his unwritten books await him.

Southwest Classics (1974: 332)

. . . transparent prose of an enduring toughness. This is the gift all writers seek—to write language that incandesces yet does not melt.

The Little Package (1964: 194)

. . . landscape and literature. These are the two things that have come to have the strongest pull on me. Not history, not biography, or memoirs, or travel, or bibliography. No. The two l's, landscape and literature. Books that combine the beauty of the land with the beauty of the language. Books in which the thing described and the language of description are in perfect register, one overlying the other, so that there is no blur. Books in which the transparent language of literature affords the reader a clear look at landscape and life. *California Librarian* (1964: 145)

What are qualities that make language live? *Feeling* is one. A writer's ability to feel life deeply, to be responsive to it. Then *power over language*, the gift to use words significantly and to form them in ways to give them meaning and impact. Also the quality of *style*, a writer's personal way with words, as intimate a part of a good writer as the size and shape of his nose. *Knowledge* is another quality that elevates writing into literature, so that the reader is memorably informed and made aware of new worlds. *Insight* is still another quality—a writer's ability to illuminate experience, to light up the dark places so that the reader sees life more clearly. And lastly what [J. Frank] Dobie calls *perspective*, so that in reading one is aware of relationships both in space and time.

The Little Package (1964: 240)

The good writer, the great writer, has what I have called the *three S's*: the power to see, to sense, and to say. That is, he is perceptive, he is feeling, and he has the power to express in language what he observes and reacts to.

The Untarnished Gold, the Immutable Treasure (1970: 3)

The timid will be frightened by his daring, the orthodox miss his true religiousness, carpers will carp, purists fuss: but . . . I will keep on reading [Robinson] Jeffers.

Robinson Jeffers: The Man and his Work (1940: ix)

What I seek in a book is information, inspiration, imagination, and a mastery of the language. That's all. How rarely they are to be found all in a single book! No period in time or special form of literature has a monopoly on these qualities. They are present in Chaucer, and they are to be found in an English writer [Lawrence Durrell] born in 1912, with a name only a few letters different from my own.

Books in My Baggage (1960: 84)

I ask more of a book than the bare bones of plot, narrative, and characters. It must breathe, be chromatic and full of murmurous overtones, so that it goes on pulsing, glowing, and echoing after it is put back on the shelf. Willa Cather's [*Death Comes for the Archbishop*] is such a book . . . and . . . justly ranks in the highest realm of American literature.   *Southwest Classics* (1974: 122)

I believe that a good work of fiction about a place is a better guide than a bad work of fact. An inspired novelist has clearer vision than a hack historian, for he can make the language say precisely what he sees and feels, which is not true of some journalists and academicians who . . . have littered the landscape with clichés.

Books West Southwest (1957: 141)

The wise writer is unconcerned about the future of his work for, as Stendhal said, a writer's books are tickets in a lottery, the drawing of which does not occur until a hundred years after his death.

Southwest Classics (1974: 257)

On Lawrence Clark Powell

I started early, but not early enough to suit me. At least that's what my mother says. According to her, when I came home after my first day in the first grade I burst out with a bitter complaint against my teacher: "Here I've been to school a whole day," I said, "and I can't read and I can't write! What's she for?"

The Alchemy of Books (1954: 97)

When I was a child, the original "Book of Knowledge" was my treasured encyclopedia. Grammar schools then made no home assignments. I read for fun. I read through my set countless times, or at least I pictured through it; even now, if I close my eyes, I can see those pages on the universe, the sun and moon and the planets. *New York Times Book Review* (1967: 2)

Two of my childhood books have remained alive for me to this day; they are the first books I can remember reading—*Grimms' Fairy Tales* and *A Child's Garden of Verses*. They do not travel with me, but I should not want to be long removed from them, and my heirs would do well to bury them with me. *Books in My Baggage* (1960: 20)

I have had *Leaves of Grass* as part of my life since childhood. There has always been a handy copy I could reach for and read in, although the first one I ever saw, the one belonging to my mother and father, puzzled me by its title: did grass have leaves? I used to stare at the back of the book, from where I lay taking a forced nap in the family library, and wonder what it was all about. I was a city boy, and the only grass I knew as a child was our carefully mown front lawn.

Poems of Walt Whitman: Leaves of Grass (1964: 2)

I grew up in South Pasadena, on the sunny side of Raymond Hill, and my time was divided between reading books in the library and raising hell in school.   *The Little Package* (1964: 193)

I discovered the Public Library in South Pasadena and had a card—its number was 3089—from age six. I was recognized as an avid reader by the librarian, dear deaf old Mrs. Nellie Keith, who waived the rule of two books to one withdrawal and let me take home as many as I could carry.

Fortune and Friendship (1968: 4)

. . . I received my B.A. from Occidental College

in the halcyon summer of 1929 . . . More than anything else I wanted to sell books, for I had majored in English under two great teachers, C. F. McIntyre and B. F. Stelter, and my approach to life was (I must confess) excessively literary and romantic. For certain books I had immense enthusiasm and I was sure that I could sell hundreds of copies of them. Instead [at A. C. Vroman, Inc.] I found myself endlessly uncrating shipments & checking invoices, with no time for reading beyond the title-page.

Recollections of an Ex-Bookseller (1950: 1–2)

I am a practicing bookman today because I was *encouraged* to develop my basic bookishness, by my mother, my town librarian, two teachers at college, a printer and a bookseller, and finally by a city librarian.   *A Passion for Books* (1958: 19)

I shall never forget my wife's response when one day in the Depression I came home from my job in a bookshop and announced my intention of becoming a librarian.

"You a librarian?" she exclaimed.

"Why not?" I asked, defensively.

"You're too lively. Besides, you read books."

The Little Package (1964: 17)

It was on April 16, 1936, that I first went to the cathedral-like UCLA Library. On my way to Goodwin's office, as hidden away as was his own nature, I stood in the octagonal rotunda, among students going their bookish ways, admired the pink tiles and creamy ceramic panels. It was then and there that I experienced a moment of truth, a sudden illumination, in which I knew that this was my destined place. That night in my journal, I wrote,

"The interview with Mr. Goodwin was brief. I found him a dignified, graying, essentially non-commital man. Yes, he said, there should be a future for you in academic library work. I did not ask nor did he say anything about an eventual job at UCLA, although I was certain that my future lay there, even as his successor."

Fortune and Friendship (1968: 55–56)

I shall also never forget the first day I reported for work at UCLA. It was February 1, 1938. Mr. Goodwin led me into the depths of the library, opened the door of a remote room packed to the walls and ceiling with books and pamphlets, showed me a table, typewriter, and chair; and still not saying a word, went out the door and left me alone with the Cowan collection—a lovely fate.

Bibliographers of the Golden State (1967: 16)

In 1938 when I went to work there [at UCLA] my salary of $135 a month represented a ten dollar a month increase over what I was making at the [Los Angeles] public library. My ambition was to make $200 a month. In my first six years at UCLA, I went up to $155 a month, and then by the grace of the Board of Regents, I jumped to $500 a month. A sense of failure still haunts me for never having made the two hundred a month.

Colorado Libraries (1984: 4)

On the first day of February 1938, I began a career at UCLA which was to keep me there twenty-eight and a half years. . . . During all of those years, even the first half dozen, when I seemed to be getting nowhere, I never wavered in my conviction that *this was the place*. Fortune and friendship brought me there at the precise time a librarian of my temperament was needed. If it was made for me, I was made for it.

Fortune and Friendship (1968: 67)

On September 4, 1940, I wrote in my journal, "I

work continually, piecing together the daily tiles which will form the mosaic of my future. I want responsibility, and the opportunity to build and work with people and ideas and books. Given the chance, I can do work of lasting value."

Fortune and Friendship (1968: 81)

It is true that I became known best as a bookman, but the record shows that I was also successful as an administrator.

I selected able people, then I gave them authority, encouragement, praise, and public recognition. I took credit for nothing that I did not do myself. And that is all I have to say about library administration.   *Fortune and Friendship* (1968: 117)

. . . Professor Grant's terse comment . . . : "He can carry his weight in books."

There is the explanation of why throughout my career as librarian and teacher, I constantly held up to beginners the importance (and the rewards) of physical contact with books. And the joy of handling them. I remember once when Bill Jackson visited the Clark Library after I had become Director, and I watched him go along the shelves, taking volume after volume into his hands, opening, glancing, then putting them back, all done swiftly with ease and grace. "Once handled, never forgotten" was his only comment—gospel words of the greatest bookman of our time.　　*Fortune and Friendship* (1968: 128)

People, librarians no exception, are forgotten. Books remain. Long after I am forgotten as man and librarian, the books I collected for UCLA will, barring cataclysm, be there in the Clark and on campus, awaiting the touch of hand, the sight of eye that brings them to life.

Fortune and Friendship (1968: 119)

The three loves I have are:
　　Collecting books
　　Keeping books (which includes reading them)
　　Giving books away
　　　　　A Passion for Books (1958: 58–59)

I have been asked how I managed to read and write so much, in addition to administration, teaching, travel, and speaking. My answer was always the same: eliminate nonessentials and gain free hours. Each must decide what for him are the nonessentials. And the second part of my answer:

marry a woman of character who will adapt, protect, and nourish with unstinting loyalty and love.   *Fortune and Friendship* (1968: 178)

I am a man of many titles and one talk . . . about books. What else is there for librarians to talk about? Machines? Master them. Techniques? Perfect them. Administration? Practice it. I bring not peace, but a book.   *Special Libraries* (1961: 295)

Statistics are not my line.

Land of Fiction (1952: ix)

I have been told by some of my more exalted library colleagues—men who live above the book-line in the arctic zone of administration—that I talk too much about books.

Books West Southwest (1957: 26)

I was asked to give a talk in Houston, Texas. And I said I would. The time passed, and the telephone rang. It was the chairman of the committee of the Women's Club of Houston. She said, "Dr. Powell, we need a title for your talk." I said: "There isn't one. I come to talk." "No," she said, "We must have a title to put in the programme and now we want it; in an hour we are going to press." Oh, I couldn't think. I said, "Well, it's going to be a kind of literary cocktail, I guess. Call it 'Shake Well and Speak.'" And we hung up. And the time passed and there I was in Houston, Texas, on the stage being introduced by the same lady who had telephoned me, who said: "Here is Dr. Powell, come all the way from Los Angeles to speak to us on Shakespeare and Keats." And I did.   *Antiquarian Bookman* (1963: 131)

I believe in books, share Milton's respect for their sacred nature, earn my living as a bookman, and seek constantly to communicate my feelings to others, by example, by the spoken and written word, by "living with books," in the words of Helen E. Haines.   *A Passion for Books* (1958: 16)

Today's supreme waster of precious time is commercial TV. I am an old-fashioned radio buff. Radio needs only ears. My eyes are a priceless asset, not to be wasted on the jackassery of commercial TV.   *Wilson Library Bulletin* (1970: 386)

Books are my lifeline. I am nourished by books fully as much as by bread and milk.
                          Books in My Baggage (1960: 171)

Books are a means of escape for me, of course they are; but deeper *into*, not farther *from* life.

Landscapes and Bookscapes of California (1958: 15)

Each man needs, seeks, and, if fortunate, finds faith and security. As a librarian I find mine among books and the infinity of service they contain.

The Little Package (1964: 38)

My reading has always been extremely personal—why deny it?—a hungry search for books to feed my own prejudices, as well as to strengthen my weaknesses, an earnest quest for verification of my own experience.

Islands of Books (1951: 54)

I read books for several reasons: the dictionary in order better to write and speak our difficult language. The encyclopedia and handbooks for definite information on various subjects. Mysteries and romances for entertainment, so-called escape from the cares of the present. Books of travel and history, either to learn more about a region I have visited or something about a land I am going to see. A few novels, based on history, true to regions and peopled by lifelike characters, combine all of these qualities, and more completely satisfy me perhaps than any other books.

Books West Southwest (1957: 18–19)

I like to read books in comfort, and my ideal reading-place is propped up in bed. Thus far I have not heard of any libraries, even the fabulous one at Princeton, which provide their readers with beds. *The Alchemy of Books* (1954: 242)

Yes, I know about bricks and boards as bookshelves. I like neither. The smaller the book the more books one can own and handle and read. I need a few thousand volumes around me as a working minimum. My study measures 9 by 9.

Bookman's Progress (1968: 176)

Unlike a public library, used by many readers, wherein the books are systematically arranged on the shelves, my private library, used only by me, is arranged according to an inner logic not obvious to my friends. *Southwest Classics* (1974: 13)

My ideal book collector is Samuel Pepys who felt both intellectual and sentimental concern for his library which he left to Magdalen College upon his death in 1703. . . . Pepys' library embodies his taste, sentiment, and passion for learning. No other library so well reveals my own feelings about the place of books in my life.

Ex Libris: Notes on My Family's Bookplates
(1984: 10–11)

I have no reading program. I read books the way a hound chases a hare—loping and spurting, twisting and turning, repeatedly distracted by the false scents which lie thick on the earth. I always read with a pencil and paper handy; for if an author of a book I like mentions other books, I am apt to heed his word and go after them. My impulse here has nothing to do with the scholar's dictum: Verify your references! I drift where the wind of my taste carries me, and if it results in my reading six or eight books at once, so much the better! *Books in My Baggage* (1960: 64)

I'm an individualist when it comes to reading. I read what I like when I like. I have yet to read *War and Peace*. It's too long. If I started it, I would miss days of work, nights of sleep; so I am saving it for my old age. *The Alchemy of Books* (1954: 98)

Always a hero worshipper, my lifelong reading has been a quest for the great ones of history and literature whose character and achievements are goals for striving and beacons for guidance. In the words of the poet, "I think continually of those who were truly great."

Southwest Classics (1974: 243)

When do I get the time to read? I take it, somewhere out of every twenty-four hours. It's a matter of choosing among a number of things. I prefer reading to bridge and golf (I've never learned to play either), I prefer reading to the movies (the peak of my passion for them came about twelve or thirteen), and reading to the *Reader's Digest*.

The Alchemy of Books (1954: 100–101)

I have always wanted to write in my books, assent or dissent as the case may be, or underlinings to enable me to return more easily to useful passages. When I was little, my mother taught me it was wrong to do this. When I became a librarian, I could not permit the public to make palimpsests of the books in my charge. Thus I was doubly deterred.

Then came the paperback revolution, licensing

the release of my inhibitions. Now I read with smoking pencil, and my paperbacks are a glorious mess of marks, checks, mystic doodles, lines both horizontal and vertical, marginalia and interlines, and end-paper addenda. Even title pages come in for it, as the typographer in me is encouraged to practice the art of design.

UCLA Alumni Magazine (1962: 18)

I know about books. I have lived with them all my life, have collected a million and a half for my university, and a few for myself. Have written some, read many; and best of all, led other people to read.

The Little Package (1964: 231)

The only way to get any reading or writing done in this environment [the Malibu] is to retreat to my study at the back of the house, pull the curtains to shut out sight of the mountains through the leaves of the olive tree, and sit facing the wall, yellow pad on my lap, blue pencil in my fist, and hope.

The Little Package (1964: 281)

I have always preferred some people to most books, and most books to some people.

Reynolds Catalogue 78 (1963: 3)

I may have been a maverick, but I was never a loner. I was always a joiner, believing I could raise more hell from inside. Don't expect everyone to like you, and don't like everyone. There's a difference between liking and loving. Although in the abstract I love my fellow men and women, I sure as hell don't like them all.

Library Journal (1983: 1427)

Catalog librarians have never cared for the titles of my books, finding them vague and unprecise. A book about books called *Islands of Books*, bore on its Library of Congress printed card the word (essays), added in parentheses after the title, as a warning I suppose to those who might check it out in search of literature about marine land masses. Another one called *Books West Southwest* contained no punctuation between the three words. The cataloger decided it needed a colon after Books. Imagine the weather report reading Wind Colon West Southwest!

Landscapes and Bookscapes of California (1958: 1)

In this technical world I never made, I practice techniques learned long ago. Mastery of that system called The Alphabet whereby I learned to read. Manipulation of the Alphabet in the act of writing. My best technical accomplishment is Typing. Back in high school days, I won a state-wide speed-typing contest as the only boy to enter. Although the three by five card is said to be obsolete, I still favor libraries with a card catalog. My first years as a librarian were spent as a bibliographical checker, and the card catalog was my security blanket. Don't take it from me!

Library Journal (1983: 1426)

Bookshops are my favorite place; their denizens my favorite people. Add libraries and librarians. My life has been divided between bookshops and libraries, has thus been spent with people animated by a love of literature, learning, and service to others. That is why it has been such a rich life.   *LCP's Book about Bookshops* (1966: 7–8)

And so, from California to Egypt to Spain and France, this conjunction of the Three L's has occurred repeatedly for me; and for the life of me, this travelling reader, this reading traveller cannot say which of the three is supreme: landscape, literature, or life. Perhaps they are really one.

The Three L's (1964: 8)

Libraries and literature, literature and libraries. How can they be separated? I went as a child to the library for books to read, for tales that took me out of myself and far away. "I should like to rise and go, where the golden apples grow." I did rise, did go, and because of books. . . . I became a librarian, I suppose . . . because it seemed a way to come closer to books, to literature, and then to bring others with me, to lead, to share.

Fortune and Friendship (1968: 129)

Seventy years ago when I was six, I got my first library card from the South Pasadena Public Library. I remember its number. God knows how many times I wrote 3089 on the book checks. That little Carnegie library was my refuge from teachers who said "No!" The librarian, dear old Mrs. Keith, said "Yes!" Like Haynes of Harvard, Nellie Keith established my lasting image of the good librarian. When she leaned down from behind the desk and reached me her hand, although neither of us knew it, that was the call to my life's work.

Library Journal (1983: 1427)

A compulsion to create, to succeed, to be recognized and praised, moved me to do what I did, and yet I was never without the knowledge of what I owed to fortune and friendship. Wherever I went, whatever I did, I sacrificed to the gods. Whoever helped me, I tried in turn to help; or if he did not need it, then I sought to help someone else in need. This law of compensation I tried always to honor, and in my teaching to impress it on my students. If one has been helped, then he must help others. If he has received, then he must give. Only by unloading some of what he has, can one make room for more.

Fortune and Friendship (1968: 213)

I was born crazy about books, and all my life has been a pleasant worsening of the state, from my earliest years in a small-town public library to my working life in great libraries all over the world and in bookshops and private collections.

A Passion for Books (1958: 16)

All my life I have traveled with books in my baggage, gone with books at my side . . . I find them as necessary as food and air.

Books in My Baggage (1960: 11)

Books have been my love from earliest years, first

as a reader, then as a seller, next as a custodian, and finally as a writer. Through books I have made friends the world around. . . . Books hold quintessential life, are realer than reality, in that they are more lasting than human life.

Fortune and Friendship (1968: xii)

. . . it would be nice to go out with book in hand. *The Little Package* (1964: 180)

Bibliography

The Abiding Legacy: Remarks on the Occasion of the Dedication of the Addition to the Mary Norton Clapp Library. Los Angeles: Occidental College, 1971.

The Alchemy of Books. Los Angeles: The Ward Ritchie Press, 1954.

At the Heart of the Matter. Los Angeles: Friends of the UCLA Library, 1957.

Bibliographers of the Golden State. Los Angeles: University of California, 1967.

Bookman's Progress: The Selected Writings of Lawrence Clark Powell. Los Angeles: The Ward Ritchie Press, 1968.

Books in My Baggage. Cleveland: World Publishing Company, 1960.

Books West Southwest. Los Angeles: The Ward Ritchie Press, 1957.

California Classics. Los Angeles: The Ward Ritchie Press, 1971; Santa Barbara: Capra Press, 1982.

Ex Libris: Notes on My Family's Bookplates. Tucson: Press on the Bajada, 1984.

Fortune and Friendship: An Autobiography. New York: R. R. Bowker Company, 1968.

From the Heartland. Flagstaff, AZ: Northland Press, 1976.

Good Reading. Los Angeles: UCLA Library, 1961.

The Human Side of Bookplates. Louise Seymour Jones. Los Angeles: The Ward Ritchie Press, 1951. (Introduction by Lawrence Clark Powell, pp. xi–xiii)

Islands of Books. Los Angeles: The Ward Ritchie Press, 1951.

Know Your Library. Los Angeles: University of California, 1954–60.

LCP's Book about Bookshops. Second Edition Unenlarged. Los Angeles: Dawson and Boswell Publishers, 1966.

Land of Fiction. Los Angeles: Glen Dawson, 1952.

Landscapes and Bookscapes of California. Berkeley: The Friends of the Bancroft Library, University of California, 1958.

Librarian-on-Leave. Collected by Everett Moore. Los Angeles: [Printed at Los Angeles City College] 1954.

The Little Package. Cleveland: World Publishing Company, 1964.

The Magpie Press Typographical Cookbook. Santa Monica, CA: The Magpie Press, 1964.

A Passion for Books. Cleveland: World Publishing Company, 1958.

Poems of Walt Whitman: Leaves of Grass. Selected by Lawrence Clark Powell. New York: Thomas Y. Crowell Company, 1964. ("Walt Whitman" by Lawrence Clark Powell, pp. 2–7)

Reynolds Catalogue 78: The West, A Holiday Roundup of Choice Books and Pamphlets. Van Nuys, CA: J. E. Reynolds, Bookseller, 1963. ("A Backward Look at Christmas Time," by Lawrence Clark Powell, pp. 1–3)

Robinson Jeffers: The Man and His Work. Revised Edition. Pasadena, CA: San Pasqual Press, 1940.

Service or Organization: Two Views—Three Responses. Tucson: University of Arizona Library, 1974. ("A Cold Look at a Hot Subject or Whose Library Is It?" by Lawrence Clark Powell, pp. 1–6)

Southwest Classics. Los Angeles: The Ward Ritchie Press, 1974; Tucson: University of Arizona Press, 1982.

Southwestern Book Trails. Albuquerque, NM: Horn and Wallace, Publishers, 1963.

A Southwestern Century. Van Nuys, CA: J. E. Reynolds, Bookseller, 1958.

The Three H's. Los Angeles: The Press in the Gatehouse, 1971.

The Three L's. Los Angeles: The Press in the Gatehouse, 1964.

UCLA/American Association of University Professors, March 5, 1959: The Library in the Expanding University.

The Untarnished Gold, the Immutable Treasure: A Report on a Book-in-Progress. (Keepsake Number 3, Library Associates of the University Library.) Davis: University of California, 1970.

William Andrews Clark Memorial Library, University of California. *Report of the Director, 1958/59*.

You, John Milton. Norman: University of Oklahoma Library, 1966.

JOURNALS

AB: Bookman's Yearbook, 1957: 44, "Book Collecting and Libraries."

ALA Bulletin, 1965 (July-August): 643–648, "Great Land of Libraries."

Antiquarian Bookman, 1963 (July 15): 131–132, "Shake Well and Speak."

Arizona Highways, 1960 (August): 6–13, "Oasis of Books."

"Books Will be Read," in *Library Association Proceedings, Papers . . . at the Harrogate Conference . . . 1957* (London: Library Association, 1957): 47–52.

California Monthly, 1963 (March): 18–20, "Home Reference Library for the College Graduate."

College and Research Libraries, 1939 (December): 97–103, "The Functions of Rare Books."

Colorado Libraries, 1984 (March): 4–8, "The Long Commitment."

"Elements of Fruitfulness," *Bulletin of the Southern California Chapter, Antiquarian Booksellers Association of America*, 1956 (November): 1–2, 5.

Library Journal, 1957 (December 15): 3159–3161, "Care and Feeding of the Bookish Administrator."

———. 1957 (December 15): 3172, "Catalysts of Knowledge."

———. 1962 (January 1): 60, "On the Grindstone."

———. 1962 (February 1): 514, "On the Grindstone."

———. 1964 (February 1): 561–565, "Education of an Educator."

———. 1983 (August): 1426–1427, "Connecting Up."

Library Quarterly, 1976 (October): 463–464, review of *Old and Rare: Thirty Years in the Book Business* by Leona Rostenberg and Madeleine B. Stern.

New York Times Book Review, 1967 (November 5): 2–3, 68–69, "Things We Need to Know."

The Rub-Off, 1958 (January-February): 2–3, "A Little Sermon on Binding."

Special Libraries, 1961 (July-August): 295–299, "Into the Mainstream."

UCLA Alumni Magazine, 1962 (March): 18–19, "One Hundred Paperbacks for the Library of a Sophisticated Family."

UCLA Librarian, 1956 (June 29): 119.

———. 1959 (January 9): 42.

———. 1960 (January 8): 36.

Wilson Library Bulletin, 1959 (February): 419–421, "Administration in One Easy Lesson."

———. 1970 (December): 384–389, "Shoe on the Other Foot: From Library Administrator to User."

About the Author

LAWRENCE CLARK POWELL was for twenty-eight years head librarian of the University of California at Los Angeles, service that led, among other things, to the undergraduate library's being named in his honor. After many years of traveling through the American Southwest and writing on the region, he moved to Tucson, Arizona, in 1971, where he is professor in residence at the University of Arizona. Among his many books are *Southwest Classics*, *Books West Southwest*, *California Classics*, *The Blue Train*, *Arizona: A Bicentennial History*, *Where Water Flows*, and *From the Heartland*.

About the Editor

JOHN DAVID MARSHALL is a member of the library faculty of Middle Tennessee State University. Among his books are *Of, By, and For Librarians*, *An American Library History Reader*, and *Louis Shores, Author-Librarian: A Bibliography*. In 1984 he received the Tennessee Library Association's Frances Neel Cheney Award for "outstanding contributions to the world of books and librarianship."

DESIGN BY CHRISTOPHER STINEHOUR

TYPE SET BY WILSTED & TAYLOR

PRINTED AND BOUND BY EDWARDS BROTHERS